AFTER THE SCARS HAVE HEALED

JOHANNA SPARROW & H. SMITH

After The Scars Have Healed

Johanna Sparrow & H. Smith

After The Scars Have Healed

Written and Copyright © 2023 by Johanna Sparrow

Edited by Sheri Guy

After The Scars Have Healed

Contents

After The Scars Have Healed

Introduction

I am a survivor, not by my own hands but by none other than the grace of God. Many people I walked the streets with did not make it, but Jesus kept me safe. The day I put God first in my life and went into covenant with him, seeking only his face, allowing him to guide me for everything, this was the day my life changed forever. No longer does the lifestyle of prostitution call out to me, or the need to do drugs or the things of the street interest me. My walk with God has been one constant, a lifeline for sure. For I know without it, I would not be here today. I have been given life in every way possible, if not a second chance, which may be hard to believe for many. For this new life, I will never look or return to those old ways that kept my foot in darkness or at death's door. After the Scars Have Healed is my story. My truth told in my own words of how life has turned out for me since being delivered and set free from a troubled life. God is my companion and drug of choice, and he has blessed me since turning to him during the worst time in my life.

It does not matter what you have done or how long you have been on the streets. You can be given a second chance and be blessed. "How did you do it, Helen?" People often ask me. I am not ashamed of my past life or how destructive I was in the streets. I tell my story wherever I go because I know someone needs to hear how to overcome trauma and that forgiveness is for all of us. After all, life is not over, even when those you love walk away from you. God's love and power when you are genuine about changing your life does show up and makes a difference for all who can see and believe. Those who know of my past also realize my relationship with God has changed my life and made me a light in a dark world.

I do not fear man and only seek to do what is suitable for my soul by seeking the face of my God. Once I started to believe, I saw more things happening in my life for the good, and the blessing that flowed was because of my relationship with my

God. The horrors of your life do not have to be your final story. You can change the ending with God in your life as I have because, with him, anything is possible.

Finding My Place in This World

Since leaving a life of hurt and pain behind, I now understand what is good for me and what is not. I have been a blessing to others, and others to me. I am no longer that broken or wounded person I believe I was all my life. The days of not wanting to live anymore are gone; thank God, I am here and here to stay. I thought I was strong because I walked the streets, but baby, I am stronger today.

Some days are easier than others, and at times, my mind for just a moment slips back to the old life I once had. I am thanking God for helping me through it all. I survived so much; sometimes, my life when I was in the streets feels like a dream. I have accomplished so much and see the blessings around me. Although I never remarried or had children, I have work, home, and two loving dogs, Buddy and the newest addition to the family, Chosen.

If you had asked me back then if I would be this blessed in my future, I would have said, "No." My life is so different today. You know what I am talking about if you read the book Helen Scars. I was on the edge of life and death. I did not care what happened to me. I was unhappy and found ways to not think about how sorry my life was. I was a taker, and I broke many hearts along the way. I did not know my place then, but now I do.

Every day is a blessing now when I wake up. My home and car are things I did not have when I walked the street. I received one gift after the other when I turned my life around. Looking at me today, you would never have known the life I lived. The old Helen is gone forever, and you will only know her if you read Helen Scars. I am healing daily, yet I never forget what I went through.

I often wonder what my life would have been like if I had never lived such a lifestyle of drugs and prostitution. I get emotional when looking back on all my pain and self-destruction. Now I know who I am and what is best for me. It took me growing up and changing my views to see the beauty in the world.

Hurricane Katrina Set Me Free

I remember doing so much on New Orleans's streets. I felt I was always surviving. I had come to terms with my life choices, and who I had become was no surprise. Before Hurricane Katrina, I did what I could to make ends meet.

Before Hurricane Katrina, I saw so many negative things happening around me. I wanted better for my life and knew I deserved it, but I did not know how to get it. Making fast money through prostitution was the only way to support my lifestyle and drug addiction.

One would not usually look at more tragedy as being set free, but for me, Hurricane Katrina transformed my life and those around me. And for some people, anything additional to what they are going through is a breaking point, but not for me. There were just more people hurting like I was. So many people around me lost everything, including their lives, during Hurricane Katrina. The New

Orleans I knew all my life was gone, but so was the Helen I used to be.

Who would have thought that with so much destruction, my life would change forever? Although I tried to keep my old lifestyle, nothing was the same. Thousands moved away from New Orleans and never returned, as did I for a little while. Some areas within my home state still look like ghost towns today. And I am blown away by so much I accomplished after Hurricane Katrina. A life of prostitution and drugs makes you not want to look in the mirror because you know you are better than that life of sin. I stayed with that lifestyle because I felt I had nothing to live for besides hurt, pain, betrayal, and the mountain of lies I would tell myself to sleep at night. Today, I rest in peace without worry. My days are good to me as I am good to myself, something I had to learn to be.

It's funny how you see the world and all its beauty when you allow yourself to live. I see the world with new eyes. Today, my scars are like the ghost town of those parts of New Orleans that Hurricane

Katrina cleared, leaving nothing standing. I see my scars from my lifestyle of drugs and prostitution similarly. I am happy I survived. It was not easy, but I did it with God's grace.

My Truth

I realized a long time ago that I was alone in this world, and I struggled with being alone daily. Who wants to be in this world alone? Although my family is large, there was so much distance. However, I am here to report that I no longer feel alone. With the change in my heart and mind came a shift in how I saw everything around me, including my family members. What family does not have issues? The larger the family, the more problems they face. I could not see much then in the way of my troubles, fears, and insecurities, but now, I know the role I played in how many things went down. I ran from myself and thought my troubles and problems would disappear in the streets, but they did not because my mind was not right. I was not bringing anything positive to my life, but my life has changed, and I can see the new me.

Today, I am learning how to appreciate my loved ones. I do not want to live in the past because it's a dark place that has never brought me joy. Lies can become the truth if you lie to yourself long enough about anything. I stopped feeling sorry for myself long ago and started embracing the infinite possibilities of who I wanted to be.

Learning to forgive myself and others is a significant part of my healing. I look back at my life and am blown away by how far I have come. Can you see me? Wanting the world to see me and not my hurt and pain was more than a question long ago; it was something I was seeking. I was nonexistent, but I stand firm today. I know who I am and my journey to getting here.

Some life lessons force you to look at yourself and make changes. I used to be guarded because I did not feel safe, not even in my skin. I am better today. I see things clearer. I no longer beat myself up for past mistakes that were out of my control. I am much more patient with myself and getting to know who I am and have chosen to be. Do I get along with everyone in my family? No, but who does?

I was one never to say the world is beautiful because, as you know, there are moments when it is not. Today, it is lovely because I can see that beauty within myself. From that, I am learning how to give that beauty to the world around me—by helping others or putting a smile on their face.

I used to tune people out when they talked to me because I did not want to hear the truth. I welcome the truth, and listening to people speak has taught me much. I am happy with who I am today. Getting to this place of peace of mind was difficult, but I am here. I love my family members even when they disagree with me.

I have come to love everyone and would do anything to help others. I was fighting not to be that person who loved everyone because I was afraid of getting hurt. No one can hurt me; I can only hurt myself. I have learned during those years I was walking the streets how to protect myself.

I am covered now by a higher power; this I know. I am okay with people not liking me or wanting me around. It no longer bothers me.

I understand my feelings, and I allow myself to feel more. No longer am I this rock hardened by life and a lack of love and acceptance. Today, I know my family loves me. People love you the best way they know how, even if it is not how you want. I understand that now.

Acceptance can be difficult. Finding your truth is one thing, but accepting that truth can be difficult. I had to embrace who and what I was at that time, I was a Black woman invisible to the world and everyone around me. Changing other's perceptions is not always easy. A change in perception that is positive will always make a person question it, and that is what makes it difficult. At first, I struggled with my new me. I no longer struggle with my recent acceptance of myself and love myself just as I am. I am far from perfect, and every day, I work hard to see the good in others as I have done with myself.

Praying For Others

It's been a long road, yet I am here. I made it. My mind sometimes takes me back to the years when I walked the streets of New Orleans that had no love for me. I was on the streets for so long that I was blind to the rest of the world, but I would eventually escape it. Now, I find myself praying for those who are still in the life I once lived. In a life where hope is nowhere to be found, love is a smiling face traded in favor of a sexual service. There are many Helens still walking the streets today. That I know has not changed much.

I can never forget the people who walked the streets with me. Some made it, and some did not. The roads could be more friendly, especially if you are used to them, but who is? Walking the streets, I met people from all walks of life who were out there for different reasons. The homeless, drug addicts, runaways, and the mentally ill, it did not matter. We were in the streets together. The streets are where you tell yourself you will rise and get that big break. They are also where many people I knew— including myself at one time—felt trapped, stuck, and out of luck.

You see people around you daily going on with life as if you do not exist. People going about their day would look at us like we were nobody's. Although it would bother me at times, I was making money. Night and day was a struggle to survive. Just a lot of broken people walking around.

I pray that the people in the streets find the strength to leave. I pray that the people still walking the streets find Christ in their lives as I have. There is no easy way of escaping the streets other than to ask for help and want to do better, but that is only easy sometimes. I am praying that God blesses me to be able to help others who need help on the streets. I know how people feel out there seeing the world they live in go by them every day. Sometimes, a smile from another person can brighten another person's day. Giving a few dollars or helping with fresh clothes or a meal can go a long way. These were things I wanted for me in between prostituting. I often made the best of my situation if I was not high on drugs.

Some people who walk the streets may have family who know they are out there, or they may not. My family knew what I was doing, and I stayed in the streets. Every person walking the streets to make money has a story to tell, and going home may not be an option. Family members look to help sometimes, especially if they have helped in the past. But no one is more tired of how and where they live than the people who have to live on the streets.

So, I pray for those people who find themselves living in the streets, and in my prayer, I ask Jesus to save them and bless them so they can be a blessing to someone else. I know how difficult living on the streets to survive can be and how it can tear you down. The streets love no one and take from you more than you are willing to give, including your life. If you have a loved one or friend who has taken to living on the streets, please reach out to them and assist them, if you can, because we all need help and to know someone cares.

Free From Drugs

Not long ago, my life revolved around drugs. I used drugs to escape my heartaches and the life I had. Not only did the drugs I used help me not to care or fear what people thought of me, but they also helped me to get through prostitution. It was clear drugs took over my soul. I needed it in my life. I was an addict, and so was my husband, who used to beat me. The thought of it alone brings back unpleasant memories. Like everything else, I survived a life of drugs. Looking back on that time. In Helen Scars, I tell you that story. I was a troubled young woman.

Being hooked on drugs does not feel good. You crave it; it is all you think about when you can't get it. It stops you in your tracks and robs you of your future. You begin to take drugs to focus and get through the day. It's the only thing that gives you back your life. And for me, this was normal. I was a drug addict.

I am free from drugs. Thank you, Jesus. I no longer need them to exist. I can focus and see purpose in my life. The things, lord, a person does when they are not able to buy drugs. You would rob and steal from anyone without care for your life or safety. There were times I wondered how I got so tied up in drugs. I must say I was around it all my life, whether in prescription form or just people on my block selling it. You could never escape it, no matter how hard you tried. It was a different time back then, and everyone was doing something to make them feel good. I guess for me. It was just a matter of time.

Do you know there would be whole families doing drugs together, hooking their loved ones individually? The issue with drugs is that you eventually want something more substantial once you start. My husband, at the time, was on heroin and hitting the streets badly for it. I was addicted to clickems. But like I said before, in my home growing up, my mother was addicted to painkillers and sleeping pills. Always something addicting us, you know. How could I escape it? As much as it was not good for me, it made what I was doing in the streets a little easier, it made me not care.

Lord, I am free from drugs. I made it. Through all of the horrors and pain, not to mention the damage I was causing myself by walking the street through the people I interacted with. I am so glad I did not lose my life. People are dying daily from drug overdoses, and I managed to escape it. I can genuinely say I gambled many times with my life in one way or another. Drugs give you a false sense of not being bothered by the troubles of your life. It made me look away from the noise in my life and provided a deadly distraction that was no doubt destructive. When I became free of drugs, it forced me to look at myself and my life's direction. I looked at my life and was not happy. Not being on drugs forced me to face that pain, and it was in my face. I had ignored my life for a long time. I was at a crossroads and forced to change for the good or stay on that path that would lead to my death. Seeing my life in shambles and out of control was eye-opening. I had issues and had to fight my mind to live.

What's it going to be, Helen? I asked myself this when trying to stop taking drugs one day. Trust me, I had no family or friends assisting me— just my bible, as odd as that may sound. From the time I picked up that bible so long ago, I put down drugs, although it was no walk in the park. For the first time, I cared and wanted to live. I cared about myself and have been caring about my life ever since. I tell people Jesus saved me. That voice had me pick up my bible and read it when I was sick after taking drugs. I pray that those who are walking the streets today get free as I have and experience the joy I have, which is a life free from drugs. It is a fantastic feeling.

Loving Life

By now, you know my story very well, especially if you read Helen's Scars, where I tell my story about how it was for me walking the streets for a dollar, strung out on drugs and prostituting. I did not think much of my life then, and why should I? I was looking more for a way out than living. You know you can beat yourself up more than anyone can with what you tell yourself. I told myself many things to escape how I felt about my life and those around me. Not feeling loved by my family was just one of many moments I had to face and make peace with if I was going to get myself out of the dark place I was living in.

Everything I have learned about myself has helped me become the person I see standing today. Yes, I know I have hurt many people along the way. Hurting others was my way of not getting hurt if you can wrap your mind around that sick way of thinking. I am happy I found a way out of it all.

I can now say I love my life. Getting to this place of love and loving myself was difficult, but I am here, and it feels terrific. I have learned how to accept myself and forgive myself. For some, that can be challenging, especially if you live in the past. I count every day as a blessing, and where I saw rain, I now see sunshine. I am blessed and sometimes blown away by how successful I have become. My trust in God is stronger than when I started. Seeking God's face kept me focused on life. I never thought I would be this person who walks around with a smile, delighted with life, and appreciative of my journey.

Although my start in this world was not good, the process it took and the journey of it are lovely. When people see me today, they can see I am different—not the Helen they once knew who would fight you anywhere and anytime. Even those around me and my family can see how happy I have become because I am free from that old life I once lived. Prostitution and drugs are in my rearview mirror. Yes, far behind me.

I am so happy to be sharing my happiness with you today. It does not matter how bad you think you have it. Someone out there is going through worse and finding a way out. I will continue to better myself through the grace of God and stay focused. Most of all, I will work daily to be a loving light to others who have found themselves overpowered in this world where everything is not as it seems. The good person you are looking to assist you should be that person you are to others. I am going to keep loving my life because life is beautiful.

I Am No Longer Drowning

At one time, I felt I could not pull myself up and out of the lifestyle I once lived. I was into so much, as I said before, looking for love, family, and respect, yet finding abuse, pain, and fear in their place. I was so down for so long; I did not know what to be up or happy was. I was looking to others for the changes I needed to create for myself.

Being overwhelmed with the pressures of this world and feeling "less than" in my family compared to the other siblings make for a dark, brewing mind. I could lie my way out of how I was feeling or even take what I wanted from others when they were not looking to better my situation. I could not see anything working for me because I was too deep and did not realize I was drowning.

I was a walking life of sin and knew it. Trust me, I was nothing nice back in the day. Life's events hardened me. It was either kill or be killed, lie or be lied to. There were no friendly people around me.

Even the ones I rolled with, you still had to watch your back. Giving up on a drowning Helen meant killing me, and, baby, I welcomed death at that time. I would fight, man; I did not care back then. I am free now.

That person, looking back on it, was lost, falling fast to a fate of corruption. Yet when you live as I did, you think you are in control of many things and that nothing can hurt you, or if you do get hurt, it's because and only because you slipped up. That's what happened, so it's your fault. There is competition in the streets more than you know, and it's not just about staying alive. No, it's about who can take, lie, and use the most to get what they want or need.

Now, that drowning person I once thought was so strong was broken and weak. Many people live on the streets, trying to survive through dirty deeds, prostitution, and drugs. An entire other world exists in plain sight of the well-established, accomplished, upstanding people or those who have decided to do things the right way. People walking the streets on drugs are drowning like I was.

Life has now been good to me, and that is because I have allowed it. I stopped blocking my happiness and looking at the rest of the world as if it was against me for what I was going through in my personal life and marriage. "The world is not all bad, no Helen," I told myself. I said to myself that all the more when I accepted Christ into my life and could get off drugs without any program assisting me. "No, Helen, there are good people in the world and people who love you and care for you. No, Helen," I told myself a thousand times.

You cannot escape who you are. It's when you give yourself that true "yes" that makes all the difference in your life, turning your world upside down. I learned to say "Yes" in places where it impacted my life. So, how about yes for a chance? Yes, Helen, you are wanted, cherished, adored.

Yes, Helen, most of all, you are no longer drowning because you are loved! Everything in my life had to change, including how I and others saw me. No was all I heard; it did not feel real even when I received a yes. What was to come behind the yes I was given? The yes I can now provide myself with means so much more to me than anything else because no one can take away my Yes. Yes, I am blessed.

My Little Blessings

Buddy and Chosen are my little blessings. I never had children. For me, they are my fur babies but my children, and I love them both. After my life changed and I began straightening up, I wanted to take care of more than myself. I had been looking out for only me in this world and did not want that anymore. Not remarrying and not having children like my brother and sisters meant that I would not have a family. I did not have to think about this much in the streets. Since my lifestyle has changed and I am in a much better place mentally and physically, it was time to bring happiness into my life.

I received Buddy in 2006, and he has been the little man in the house, a welcomed child. And in 2021, I received my little girl, Chosen, from my nephew. We are a family, and I love them. They are my children, my little ones. I could not share my healing without discussing my two little blessings.

Sometimes, they can be a handful, but I love every moment with them. They keep me smiling. I am happy to experience this moment with them.

I am a worried mother when anything is wrong with Buddy or Chosen. Taking them to the vet or buying their favorite toys feels so good. They have their special days when I make them their favorite meal. Yes, baby, I cook for my babies. Broiled Steak or chicken, rice, and vegetables are what I make for them. They are my children, and I treat them as such. I enjoy having them in my life. They are my little blessings that I thank God for every day.

I am happy when I am home and spending time with my babies. I am just as protective of them as they are of me.

Every day, I am amazed by my life and the person I have become. As I said, getting to this place was not easy, but it was necessary. My scars heal; when I laugh and play with my little ones, the wounds do not exist. The joy I feel from seeing their faces when I wake up and before I go to bed is why they are my blessing. The little things always bring about the most peace in your life. They are my little guardian angels because their faces and need for me are priceless.

I talk about them everywhere I go. What mother isn't proud of her children? My babies just so happen to be fur babies. Taking care of Buddy and Chosen is a blessing. I cannot see myself without either one of them. They make me smile and fill my day with laughter even when they are not getting along. We are our own little family, you know.

Things that would not have been important to me long ago are today, like family. Everything is new to me; I can love after so much pain and hurt, and I never thought I could. I am different as a mom—at least, that is how I feel with my little man Buddy and little girl Chosen. Today, I cannot imagine my life without them. They are my little blessings.

Because Of Prayer

Since prayer has changed my life for the better, those dark clouds are nowhere in sight. I was once not a believer in how powerful prayer was until I did it: I prayed for help. It works and is still working in my life. I pray for the people around me daily. I am standing on what got me to where I am today: reading God's word, prayer, and my faith. Nothing more. No one needs to remind me where I came from. I already know and will never return.

Because of prayer, I am stronger than I have ever been. Because of worship, I smile more. I see the world with new eyes, not the dead eyes I used to have. If you told me back in the days when I lived walking the streets looking for Johns and heavy on drugs, I would have cut you for playing with me. I would have laughed and walked away because I knew my life was going nowhere. Because of prayer and the willingness to change and seek change, I now have been given a second chance.

It may not look like much to you, but for me, it's a lot more than I could ever imagine or want. I still see some people today when driving down the road, looking and living the way I used to look and live. I wonder if they know they can get out of it—they can change and be blessed. Do they know that prayer is real? I am a living example of it.

I pray for the world and everyone in it that they may be, whoever they are, given a second chance to see the world I now see with new eyes. I will continue being a blessing to my family, friends, and all who know my struggle.

Only some people want to see your blessings or you smiling. Some smile at you, even if they don't believe in you, but that is alright. If you come from the streets and have lived a difficult life as I did, know you can change. You can be happy. You can find peace through prayer and seeking God's face, as he is the only one who can help you out of the life you are living.

I COULD STAND TALL when I stopped trusting man and looking for everyone else to help me instead of allowing myself and seeking the strength to do so through prayer.

Someone may be reading this now, feeling like the world is falling on them and there is no way out. You feel so alone. Trust me when I tell you that you are not alone. God sees everything. If you want a new start in your heart, it's yours to have. No one is perfect in this world. We all have something that we have had to deal with and even struggle to let go. I just knew how deep I was in the rabbit hole.

Today, that life and world seem so long ago. It sometimes shocks me during my quiet time when I think of the things I endured on the streets to survive. The lies I told myself to stay on the streets were sometimes better than my life at home. Those days of not feeling loved by my family are far behind me nowadays. The thoughts of feeling lost and alone are no longer my daily thoughts. I have come full circle, knowing who I am and why I survived where others did not.

Prayer for me is what keeps me out of my head. There is beauty in everything; even the ugly moments in life have moments of beauty that bring you to a place where you will either fight to survive or give in and give up. I've learned how to fight past my fears and hurt, not to mention the pain that took me by storm. Yet I ask, was it all worth it? Through my troubled life, I found one thing to be true and that is your scars can healed. I needed to believe in something bigger than myself. I lost belief in all that I was and could be. I hit the bottom of life and wanted to remain there despite my tears. Looking back over my life, prayer and the belief that I had a purpose was my way of facing my life, like looking through a mirror. I could then focus on myself. My life was not the sweetest nor the prettiest; it was no doubt survival. In that mirror, looking at myself while holding my bible, I prayed and cried and cried and prayed like the world was over. My soul cried out for help, and my mind reached for something to grip.

Through prayer, I stopped fighting myself and who I was. I stopped looking for a way out, looking for death, and started living. I thought desiring death was easy; I had it all wrong. Living with purpose and prayer was easier and when I changed my heart, life became more manageable.

I thank God for all my pain, heartbreak, and struggles because they have brought me more blessings than I can count. I pray my story inspires you, whoever and wherever you are. And never forget that Jesus loves you, and you can do everything through him. If my scars can healed, so can yours.

H. Smith today.

Thank you for reading my story and God bless you.

My Favorite Bible Scripts

Ephesians 3:20

Now to Him who is able to do exceedingly abundantly above all that we ask or think, according to the power that works in us.

Deuteronomy 31:6

Be strong and courageous. Do not fear or be in dread of them, for it is the Lord your God who goes with you. He will not leave you or forsake you.

Ephesians 2:4-5

But because of his great love for us, God, who is rich in mercy, made us alive with Christ even when we were dead in transgressions—it is by grace you have been saved.

Philippians 4:13

I can do all things through him who strengthens me.

Isaiah 40:31

But they who wait for the Lord shall renew their strength; they shall mount up with wings like eagles; they shall run and not be weary; they shall walk and not faint.

Isaiah 41:10

Fear not, for I am with you; be not dismayed, for I am your God; I will strengthen you, I will help you, I will uphold you with my righteous right hand.

Exodus 15:2

The Lord is my strength and my song, and he has become my salvation; this is my God, and I will praise him, my father's God, and I will exalt him.

1 Chronicles 16:11

Seek the Lord and His strength; seek His presence continually!

Ephesians 2:8–9

For by grace you have been saved through faith

Psalm 32:1

" Blessed is the one whose transgressions are forgiven, whose sins are covered."

2 Corinthians 12:9–10

But he said to me, "My grace is sufficient for you, for my power is made perfect in weakness."

2 Corinthians 12:8-9

Three times I pleaded with the Lord to take it away from me. But he said to me, "My grace is sufficient for you, for my power is made perfect in weakness." Therefore I will boast all the more gladly about my weaknesses, so that Christ's power may rest on me.

2 Thessalonians 2:16

May our Lord Jesus Christ himself and God our Father, who loved us and by his grace gave us eternal encouragement and good hope,

2 Peter 3:9

The Lord is not slow in keeping his promise, as some understand slowness. Instead he is patient with you, not wanting anyone to perish, but everyone to come to repentance.

1 Peter 5:10

And the God of all grace, who called you to his eternal glory in Christ, after you have suffered a little while, will himself restore you and make you strong, firm and steadfast.

2 Timothy 2:1-3

1 You then, my son, be strong in the grace that is in Christ Jesus. **2** And the things you have heard me say in the presence of many witnesses entrust to reliable people who will also be qualified to teach others. **3** Join with me in suffering, like a good soldier of Christ Jesus.

Matthew 5:7

Blessed are the merciful, for they will be shown mercy.

Psalm 145:9

The Lord is good to all; he has compassion on all he has made.

1 Chronicles 16:34

Give thanks to the Lord, for he is good; his love endures forever.

Psalm 100:5

For the Lord is good and his love endures forever;
his faithfulness continues through all generations.

Luke 1:50

His mercy extends to those who fear him, from generation to generation.

Jude 1:2

Mercy, peace and love be yours in abundance.

Daniel 9:9

The Lord our God is merciful and forgiving, even though we have rebelled against him.

2 John 1:3

Grace, mercy and peace from God the Father and from Jesus Christ, the father's Son, will be with us in truth and love.

Psalm 130:1-2

Out of the depths I cry to you, Lord; Lord, hear my voice. Let your ears be attentive to my cry for mercy.

2 Samuel 22:26

To the faithful you show yourself faithful, to the blameless you show yourself blameless.

1 John 1:9

"If we confess our sins, he is faithful and just and will forgive us our sins and purify us from all unrighteousness."

Ephesians 1:7

"In him we have redemption through his blood, the forgiveness of sins, in accordance with the riches of God's grace."

Colossians 1:13-4

"For he has rescued us from the dominion of darkness and brought us into the kingdom of the Son he loves, in whom we have redemption, the forgiveness of sins."

After The Scars Have Healed

Made in the USA
Monee, IL
29 September 2023